HOWLING WOLF

A Cheyenne Warrior's Graphic Interpretation of His People

HOWLING WOLF

A Cheyenne Warrior's Graphic Interpretation of His People

by
Karen Daniels Petersen

with an Introduction by
John C. Ewers

AMERICAN WEST PUBLISHING COMPANY
PALO ALTO, CALIFORNIA

Dedicated to Sidney

Acknowledgements

The drawings of Howling Wolf have been made available for publication through the courtesy of Mrs. A. H. (Anna Bourke) Richardson, owner of the sketchbook and daughter of Captain John G. Bourke, who early recognized the value of the drawings and preserved them. Photographs of the drawings were obtained through the cooperation of the Joslyn Art Museum, Omaha, where the sketchbook was deposited. To these and to the many others who have assisted in a multitude of ways, the author offers her sincere thanks. The American Philosophical Society, Penrose Fund, provided a grant permitting the necessary research. The sketchbook was brought to the author's attention by Mrs. Charles T. (Jeanne) Snodgrass, and analysis of the drawings was facilitated by Miss Mildred Goosman, Western Collections, Joslyn Art Museum. Manuscripts in the United States Military Academy Library (J. Thomas Russell) helped materially in tracing the history of the sketchbook. Study of the other Howling Wolf pictures was permitted by the Field Museum (George I. Quimby), the Massachusetts Historical Society (Stephen T. Riley), Yale University's Beinecke Library (Archibald Hanna), and Hampton Institute (Miss Eleanor A. Gilman and James A. Paige). The last two institutions opened their archives for a study of the artist's life, as did the Cheyenne-Arapaho Agency (James M. Hays, Jr.), the National Archives (Robert Kvasnicka and Garry D. Ryan), the Smithsonian Institution's Office of Anthropology (Mrs. Margaret Blaker and Dr. S. H. Riesenberg), and the Oklahoma Historical Society (Mrs. Louise Cooke and Mrs. Rella Looney). Biographical data were furnished by the artist's son, William Howling Wolf (with Mrs. Charles Curtis interpreting) and by Edmund L. G. Zalinsky. The family of General Richard H. Pratt, particularly Edgar N. Hawkins and Mrs. S. Clark Seelye, generously made available for study the papers of "Captain" Pratt.

Dr. Ewers gratefully acknowledges permission to reproduce in his Introduction pictures from: **A Preliminary Historical Outline for the Northwestern Plains** by William Mulloy (1958); the Smithsonian Institution; the Northern Natural Gas Company; the Joslyn Art Museum; **Blackfeet Crafts** by John C. Ewers; and the Collection of the Indian Arts and Crafts Board, United States Department of the Interior.

Library of Congress Catalog Card Number 68-23107

CONTENTS

Introduction by John C. Ewers

PLAINS INDIAN PAINTING

The History and Development of an American Art Form

HOWLING WOLF, restless son of the Cheyenne chief Eagle Head, hunted buffalo and fought enemy tribesmen and white soldiers in the Indian Wars on the Southern Plains before 1875. But his claim to remembrance rests neither on his prowess as a hunter nor on his achievements as a warrior. Rather it is based upon his eloquence as a story teller—as an able recorder of the history and customs of his own people, not in words but in a series of brilliantly colored pictures, executed shortly after the buffalo were exterminated and the fighting Cheyenne pacified. In his reliance upon graphic art as a medium to tell his story, Howling Wolf followed a Plains Indian tradition that was old long before he was born.

Exactly how old we cannot be sure because so

Fig. A: Before the Plains Indians acquired horses, warriors carried painted body-shields—as illustrated in this prehistoric vignette from Pictograph Cave, Montana.

5

little evidence has survived. On the plains east of the Rockies, Indians may have been painting crude representations of men and animals on rawhide shields and the inner surfaces of buffalo robes thousands of years ago. We do know that their buffalo-hunting descendants were creating primitive picture-writings on rocks and hides when the first white explorers entered their hunting grounds. Some Indians had already begun to draw and paint on paper for the edification of whites a half century before the buffalo were exterminated, and twentieth-century, reservation-born Plains Indian artists are still active today. The styles, themes, and functions of this art have changed over the years, but the tradition survives.

The primitive art that remains to us—Indian pictures painted on cave walls or incised on vertical rock surfaces at many widely scattered localities from Alberta to Texas—can rarely be dated pre-

Fig. B: Incised petroglyphs at Writing-on-Stone, Alberta, Canada.

cisely, and only a few can be assigned unquestionably to prehistoric times. Archaeologists seem to agree that some of the paintings in Pictograph Cave, 15 miles south of Billings, Montana, were created during the late Prehistoric Period, which some would date from about 500 A.D. to 1800 A.D. in that area. Noteworthy among these old pictures are a number of red, black, and white renderings of men bearing large, circular shields, which appear to conceal the warriors' entire bodies and upper legs. These shields are comparable in size to those that David Thompson, the early fur trader, tells us were carried by Blackfoot warriors in their battles with the Shoshoni on the Northwestern Plains during the second quarter of the eighteenth century, and before the Blackfoot acquired horses. They were more than three feet in diameter, and large enough to protect the entire person of a squatting or bent-legged footman from the arrows of his Indian enemies. On a number of the shields depicted in Pictograph Cave are pictured human or animal-like figures, which probably represented the spirit-helpers that the individual shield-bearers had acquired through sought visions or in dreams. (See Figure A.)

Farther north, at Writing-on-Stone, in the Milk River Valley of Southern Alberta, are numerous Indian pictures incised in soft sandstone bluffs. Here we find a few warriors bearing large shields like those of Pictograph Cave, but others are on horseback and carry guns. (See Figure B.)

In September, 1805, Francois Larocque, the first white man to leave a written account of his travels in the Yellowstone Valley, saw a large, white, perpendicular rock on which three horsemen fighting three footmen were painted in red. This was ten months before William Clark, of the Lewis and Clark Expedition, descended the Yellowstone on his return from the Pacific Coast, saw this rock landmark, and named it Pompey's

Pillar. Although Pompey's Pillar is less than fifty miles from Pictograph Cave, the painting Larocque saw on it must have been more recent than the shield-bearing footmen on the cave walls. It was almost certainly of the eighteenth century, executed between the time Indians of this region acquired European horses and the first appearance of a white explorer in the Yellowstone Valley.

On May 20, 1808, Captain José Agabo, a member of a Spanish military expedition from San Antonio to Santa Fe, while passing through the country of the Comanche in northwestern Texas, discovered a large cave "painted with various colours and figures by the Indians." We do not know whether these paintings were made by Comanche artists or earlier occupants of the Southern Plains. We do know that one of the earliest Comanche specimens preserved in museum collections is a painted shield of about 1830 on which appear two monochrome human figures, one black, the other yellow. In their circular and featureless heads, rectangular bodies, linear arms extending to three outstretched fingers, and linear legs and feet, these figures resemble some of those appearing in the numerous undated rock paintings of Texas. (See Fig. C.)

From the time of Coronado (1541), explorers and traders on the Great Plains made repeated, brief references to buffalo robes painted by Indians. Some of the Indian robes were painted in geometric designs by the women. Others were the work of men, and pictured heroic deeds in the life of the wearer—the coups he had counted in war. These pictorial records were proudly worn by successful warriors among the Plains tribes during the early decades of the nineteenth century.

The best-documented example of the traditional military art appears on a buffalo robe collected by Lewis and Clark at the Mandan villages on the Missouri and sent by them to President Jefferson in the spring of 1805. This painting portrays a battle fought about the year 1797. The twenty mounted warriors and forty-four footmen in combat are scattered over the inner surface of the robe, some armed with bows and arrows, lances, and shields, others with tomahawks or firearms. The figures are all outlined in dark brown. Some are filled in with flat colors—brown, blue-green, red, or yellow.

A detail of the robe shows the characteristic features of this art style. (See Figure D.) The men's heads are featureless knobs; their necks sit upon elongated rectangular bodies, from which extend linear arms, some bent. The legs

Fig. C: A Comanche shield of about 1830.

are relatively short and bent at the knees. Hands and feet are small and lack definition. No attempt was made to portray clothing. Notice that the mounted warriors do not straddle their horses—either they have no legs at all or both legs are shown on the near side of the horse. The horses, too, have neither eyes nor mouths, and their upper legs are thick, while the lower ones are mere lines. The horses' hoofs are hook-shaped extensions of their legs.

This is a good example of traditional Plains Indian painting, an aboriginal art untouched by stylistic influences from the white man's world. The primitive artist showed little interest in anatomical details. He was content to portray the general characteristics of the human form—the roundness of the head, straightness of the limbs, and the bilateral symmetry of the body. He had little interest in relative scale. Notice that some of his footmen are considerably taller than his horses. His work shows no concern with color modeling or with such concepts as foreshortening or perspective. And his figures float freely over the surface of the robe without any attempt being made to show the geographical setting in which the battle took place.

The term "picture writing" aptly describes the form and function of this primitive art. The creator of such works was as much a historian as an artist. Indeed esthetic considerations may have been secondary to the artist's concern for recording the memorable accomplishments of his own military career and those of his fellow tribesmen. He probably outlined his figures with the point of a stick and filled in the outlines of some figures by spreading flat colors with a porous bone tool. Probably he used a separate stick or bone for each color.

Before 1830 a few Plains Indians gained some firsthand knowledge of white artists' techniques and their concern for realistic portraiture. Dele-

Fig. E: Four Bears, a Mandan chief, fighting a Cheyenne. This autobiographical watercolor on paper was executed by Four Bears with the encouragement of the Swiss artist, Karl Bodmer, in 1834.

gations of prominent Indians visited Santa Fe, San Antonio, and Mexico City. Others traveled to St. Louis, New Orleans, Washington, and the larger cities of the East. A small group of Osage spent more than two years touring the cities of Europe. And we know that some of those Indians sat for their portraits by such highly skilled artists as Charles Willson Peale, Charles B. J. F. de Saint-Mémin, Chester Harding, Charles Bird King, and John Neagle.

During this same period explorers of the Great

Fig. D: A Mandan buffalo-robe painting acquired by Lewis and Clark and sent to Thomas Jefferson in 1805. The Mandan, like many other Plains Indians, possessed an artistic tradition long before the arrival of Lewis and Clark.

lack any paintings known to have been the work of those who had visited the centers of civilization, or studied illustrated books. Yet during the decade of the 1830's, a few Indians began to draw and paint in the white man's medium of pencil and watercolors on paper for whites. And white artists who visited the plains to paint Indians encouraged the native artists by providing them with both the example of their own works and the unfamiliar materials. In some instances these skilled exponents of an alien artistic tradition may also have suggested to the Indian artists some of the subjects to depict.

During the summer of 1832 George Catlin gained a reputation as a medicine man among the Mandan because of his ability to "make human beings" in two dimensions. According to Catlin's account, the Indians were particularly impressed by his rendering of his sitters' eyes, which the awestruck redmen thought "followed them" as they studied Catlin's portraits from different angles. Catlin was followed on the Upper Missouri by the technically superior Swiss artist, Karl Bodmer. During his winter's stay at nearby Fort Clark in 1833–34, Bodmer gave paper, pencils, and watercolors to at least two prominent Mandan Indians, whose portraits both he and Catlin had painted, and encouraged them to paint for him.

One of these earliest recorded Plains Indian paintings in the white man's medium is shown in Figure E. It is the work of Four Bears, the second chief and most prominent warrior among the Mandan at the time. He was a favorite of both Catlin and Bodmer and had spent many days and nights watching Bodmer paint in his makeshift studio at Fort Clark. Although this picture depicts a traditional theme, the artist's record of one of his outstanding coups—the killing of a Cheyenne chief with a knife in hand-to-hand combat—the style is a far cry from the earlier Mandan paint-

Plains began to show illustrated books to the Indians. At Engineer Cantonment on the Missouri (above present-day Omaha), scientists of the Long Expedition showed pictures to visiting Indians during the winter of 1819–20, and reported: "The Indians, almost all of them, delight to look over engravings, particularly those which represent animals; they are not soon fatigued when employed in this way."

These first acquaintances with white men's art may have influenced Plains Indian artists, but we

ing collected by Lewis and Clark. Gone are the knoblike heads, the stick figures, the distorted proportions, the lack of detail. In both figures the facial features, including eyes, are sharply defined. The bodily proportions are realistic, and both legs and arms are fleshed out. And the details of headgear, body costume, and ornaments are shown with painstaking care. Like the works of Bodmer himself, this picture was first drawn in pencil and then developed in watercolor. Can there be any doubt that Four Bears, working in an unfamiliar medium, was trying to follow the example of his friend and teacher, Karl Bodmer?

Other white artists had proteges among other Indian tribes during the second quarter of the nineteenth century. At the fur traders' rendezvous on Green River during the summer of 1837, the European-trained Baltimore artist, Alfred Jacob Miller, encouraged Little Chief, a prominent Shoshoni chief, to depict for him scenes from his war experiences. Miller noted that this Indian tried to paint with the stick end of his brush rather than with the bristles, and showed

his indifference to perspective by picturing all four legs of horses on one side.

A decade later the artist-priest Father Nicholas Point, while engaged in pioneer Christian mission work among the Blackfoot and Gros Ventres near Fort Lewis on the Upper Missouri, provided an Indian with paper and colors, and encouraged him to paint a series of fascinating watercolors (primarily in blacks and browns) portraying an Indian's view of the life of the traders at the fort. The native artist's concern for proportion and for the details of costume may reflect the influence of the good Father's own painting. Yet the works show such characteristic marks of Plains Indian painting as the rendering of horsemen with both legs on one side of their mounts.

At Fort Union, near the mouth of the Yellowstone, in February, 1852, the Swiss artist Rudolph Friederich Kurz argued the relative merits of the two artistic traditions—the European and the Plains Indian—with a Sioux to whom he had supplied pen and ink and drawing paper. The Sioux found Kurz's method of picturing a rider

Fig. G: Traditional styles of Indian drawing have survived down to our times. These Blackfoot pictograph signatures were done for the author in 1943. From left to right: Rides at the Door, Weasel Tail, Takes a Gun, and Chewing Black Bones.

astride "not at all satisfactory," pointing out "you see, a man has two legs." Like other traditional Plains Indian artists, this Sioux did not draw from models, and he was not concerned that the far leg of a horseman, pictured from the side, is concealed by the horse's body.

In Kurz's time Indians of the Upper Missouri still wore painted buffalo robes. (See Figure F.) However, this custom had already been abandoned in favor of trade blankets by the Osage and other tribes nearer St. Louis, and tended to become obsolete among the more distant tribes during the next two decades. The Earl of Southesk, writing in 1859, observed: "The Sioux, of all Indians, are those who most keep up their old mode of dress; the Blackfoot and the rest are all rapidly adopting blankets and capots, and giving up the beautifully painted robes of their forefathers. The few painted robes that are made are inferior in workmanship to those of days gone by."

Nevertheless, traditional ways of rendering both human and animal forms persisted among the Blackfoot. During the 1940's I obtained examples of the ingenious pictographic signatures some of my elderly Piegan and Blood Indian informants used to draw to convey information to fellow members of their horse-raiding parties when they became separated in the time of their youth. Four of these very simple, yet effective, identifying symbols are reproduced as Figure G.

Following the Indian wars of the plains in the 1870's, Indian artists found a new clientele among the army officers who had fought against them and were interested in seeing the Indians' side of the conflict pictured in watercolors, pen and ink, or colored pencils. Colonel Richard Irving Dodge was impressed by the fact that a degree of skill in drawing was shared by so many Indians. Probably he did not exaggerate very much when he wrote: "All draw, and though

Fig. F: Hidatsa Indian
wearing a painted buffalo robe, 1851.
A field sketch by the Swiss artist Rudolph F. Kurz.

11

entirely without knowledge of perspective, all draw quite as well as the average of whites. If one wants Indian pictures, there is no need to hunt a special artist. All he has to do is to give some paper and a few colored pencils to any middle-aged warrior.'' Drawings by Indians of those tribes that had been most consistently hostile to the whites were in greatest demand. And judging from extant collections, Sioux, Cheyenne, and Kiowa veterans of the Indian wars supplied the greatest number of pictures.

A most unusual colony of artists developed at old Fort Marion, St. Augustine, Florida, where more than seventy men from five hostile tribes of the Southern Plains were imprisoned from 1875 to 1878. Most of these Indians were young men, and their humanitarian jailer, Captain Richard H. Pratt (who later founded the famed Carlisle Indian School in Pennsylvania) believed they could be made into useful and productive citizens if given direction and the opportunity to develop their native abilities. Recognizing their interest in drawing and painting, he provided them with paper, pencils, and colors, and offered them an opportunity to produce art works for sale to whites. More than a third of these ''Florida boys'' participated in Pratt's art program, and hundreds of examples of their works are preserved in widely scattered public and private collections.

Their subject matter ranged widely from nostalgic memories of events and of tribal life on the open plains to pictures of Fort Marion and the seagoing ships they saw in Florida. One of the most able among these artists was Making Medicine, a Cheyenne in his early thirties, described as a ''ringleader'' among the hostile Cheyenne at the time of his arrest in the Indian Territory. His delicately colored pencil drawings are remarkable for their decorative quality. His ''On the War Path'' (Figure H), a page from a book of drawings executed in 1875, is traditional in theme and possesses the flatness and free-floating qualities of the old hide paintings. But working in this white-man's medium—with precise drawing instruments on a smooth paper surface—Making Medicine achieved effects that were impractical in the old picture writing. In his portrayal of the running horse in a rocking-horse pose—both front and hind legs extended—he was employing a convention used also by white artists in sporting prints, and one that was gaining wide acceptance among Plains Indian artists.

Other artists of this group sought to fill their rectangular sheets with more complicated scenes after the fashion of the white illustrator. And many of their works have those qualities of quaintness often found in the efforts of ambitious folk artists whose reach exceeds their grasp of the usual principles of composition, relative scale, and perspective.

One of the prisoners, Howling Wolf (also a Cheyenne), continued to make pictures after his release in 1878. On his return to his homeland in what is now Oklahoma, he found that the old ways of his people had changed markedly during his absence from the plains. The buffalo—long the staff of life for the Cheyenne—was gone. The warlike Cheyenne had been pacified. Gone were the freedoms of the old roaming life in picturesque encampments of painted tipis. Indians were occupying houses and standing in line to receive government rations.

Possessed of a keen historical sense, Howling Wolf sat down to reconstruct on paper significant scenes in the cultural history of his own people before they settled down to the monotony of reservation life. His series of twelve pen and watercolor sketches, collected by the able soldier-ethnologist, Captain John G. Bourke, is unique among the works of Plains Indian artists

12

Fig. H: "On the Warpath," by Making Medicine. Like Howling Wolf, Making Medicine was a Cheyenne hostage held at Fort Marion, Florida, in the mid-1870's.

subjects must have been derived from the oral history of his tribe. And as might be expected, these scenes contain a few anachronisms, for the oral traditions probably were more fragmentary than the artist's compositions.

The majority of Howling Wolf's scenes, however, are of pure Cheyenne genre, depicting aspects of the tribal life he had known in his youth. Here are the Cheyenne of the 1860's and early -70's hunting the buffalo and antelope, preparing for and returning from war, performing the sacred sun dance and other ceremonies, enjoying a horse race, and dressed in their best for courtship. Howling Wolf, the folk artist, rendered even the most complex scene with naive confidence, uninhibited by any consciousness of his limitations as an illustrator.

To me the most informative of these pictures is Howling Wolf's semi-diagrammatic rendering of an Indian horse race. (See Plate Nine, page 55.) Both George Catlin and Paul Kane had painted the Plains Indian horse race, but neither of their works tell us as much about how the race was run as does Howling Wolf's watercolor. The hoof prints trace the race course—across a stream and around a hill and back to the place of beginning. Judges standing on the hill make sure that neither rider in this match race takes a short cut while out of sight of the spectators assembled near the finish line. Near the spectators are the horses and other valuables wagered by the Indians on the outcome of the event (betting added to the Indians' enthusiasm for this popular sport). I find that Howling Wolf's record of the Plains Indian horse race graphically substantiates numerous descriptions of these races told me by elderly Indians a quarter of a century ago.

The most prominent Indian artist of the early reservation period was Sitting Bull, the famous Hunkpapa Sioux chief. He repeatedly pictured his coups in intertribal wars and in fights with

of the period. His first three pictures attempt to portray important scenes and events in the long-ago history of his tribe—their first acquisition of horses from the Kiowa, of firearms from a white trader, and a view of the settlement on the Upper Missouri before the Cheyenne abandoned corn cultivation in semi-permanent villages of earth-lodges in favor of the nomadic life of buffalo hunters. Howling Wolf's knowledge of these

13

whites, but carefully avoided pictorial references to the much-disputed battle with Custer. His autobiographical drawing of counting coup on a Crow warrior may show the influence of Rudolph Cronau, a German artist-correspondent who gave Sitting Bull drawing lessons. (See Figure I.) The heavy horse with modeled rump possesses a three-dimensional quality lacking in the horses executed by other Plains Indian artists of the time.

Younger but still unschooled Indians carried the pictorial art tradition into the twentieth century. Encouraged by collectors, some artists seem to have transferred stylistic characteristics developed in drawing on paper to paintings on elkskins, or buffalo hides when they could be ob-

tained. Silverhorn (1861–1941), a Kiowa artist, received encouragement from both the professional ethnologist James Mooney and the amateur, Captain Hugh L. Scott. The portraitist E. A. Burbank near the turn of the century gave lessons to Silverhorn, whom he regarded as "the finest artist among the Kiowas. If he had had an art training in youth, he would doubtless have made himself an artist of no ordinary ability."

The revival of interest in Plains Indian pictorial art, which had found little encouragement on or off the reservations during the first quarter of the present century, dates from 1928, when fieldworkers on the Kiowa Reservation near Anadarko, Oklahoma, recognized that a group of talented boys were attempting to picture themes

Fig. I: "Killing a Crow Indian," from a pictorial autobiography executed by the celebrated Sitting Bull in 1881.

Fig. J: Raiding for horses, as pictured on elkskin by an unnamed Sioux artist, about 1890.

from Indian art. They needed encouragement and the guidance of a sympathetic and trained artist, and they found it in Oscar Jacobson, head of the School of Art at the University of Oklahoma, who accepted the Kiowa boys as special students. Without telling these boys what to depict or showing them how to draw and paint, Jacobson encouraged them to use Indian themes and to develop their own styles based upon a knowledge of the Plains Indian tradition of pictorial art. The "five Kiowa boys"—Monroe Tsa-to-ke, Stephen Mopope, James Auchiah, Jack

Fig. K: "Dancer," a watercolor by Archie Blackowl, a Cheyenne, in the mid-1940's.

Hokeah, and Spencer Asah—progressed rapidly. Some of their works were exhibited at the Exposition of Indian Intertribal Arts in New York in 1930, where thousands of white Americans first saw fine Indian work exhibited as art. Their work was also shown in international exhibitions abroad, where it received high praise—as art.

The change in the Administration of Indian Affairs with the appointment of John Collier as Commissioner in 1932 led to the encouragement of Indian art as one of the avowed objectives of a new policy. At the Santa Fe Indian School classes were opened for promising Indian artists under the skilled guidance of Dorothy Dunn (Kramer). She has told me that she assembled photographs of works Indians had done in the past for her students to examine, and that the older piece that was a special favorite with some of her Plains Indian students was a Sioux painting on elkskin, executed about 1890. A detail of the upper left corner of this painting, depicting with simple yet graceful clarity the stealing of horses by a war party, is shown in Figure J.

During the depression years some of the new group of schooled Plains Indian artists found employment painting murals for Federal Buildings—the cafeteria of the new Department of the Interior Building in Washington, parlors and gymnasiums in Indian schools, post office lobbies, the entrance lobby to the Museum of the Plains Indian at Browning, Montana, and the like. Some of the earliest graduates are still active artists, and a number of them are teaching, helping to develop new generations of Indian artists.

For inspiration many of the schooled artists turned back to the cultures of their tribes in the past days of glory, and selected aspects of the old way of life for pictorial interpretation. They became pictorial historians, like Howling Wolf, picturing a life they had never experienced themselves. Others turned to the most colorful

Fig. L: "Shunka Wakan Dance," a casein on illustration board, by Oscar Howe, Yanktonai Sioux, 1962.

Fig. M: "Of the Owl's Telling," gouache on illustration board, by the Kiowa-Comanche, Blackbear Bosin, 1965.

18

survival of the old life—the Indian dance, the subject of many modern Indian paintings. The watercolor in Figure K is one of them. Its creator, Archie Blackowl, a descendant of the Cheyenne chief Roman Nose, was a winner of the Intertribal War Dance competition at Gallup. This single dancing figure may be traditional in its stark outlining of a single man against a blank background. But it differs markedly from the works of the earlier artists in its schooled draftsmanship and combination of realistic and decorative elements.

A major source of encouragement to Indian pictorial artists since 1946 has been the Annual Indian Artists Exhibition at the Philbrook Art Center in Tulsa, a competitive show to which artists from many North American tribes have contributed during the past twenty-one years. This exhibition has sought to foster innovation and experimentation with new media and techniques, as well as new subject matter, and to discourage unimaginative repetition of old styles and themes. Some modern Indian artists have moved so far in the direction of abstraction that their works have all but lost their Indian identity. But many artists have experimented ingeniously without breaking ties with their Indian artistic heritage.

Plains Indians, in competition with Indian artists from other cultures, have won their share of the highest awards at Tulsa. One of the most successful exhibitors over the years has been Oscar Howe, winner in 1966 of the show's first Special Award for sustained creative productivity. A Yanktonai Sioux, a graduate of the Santa Fe School in 1938, and an overseas veteran of World War II, Howe has consistently gone back to aspects of Sioux life in buffalo days for his themes. His "Shunka Wakan Dance" (the old Horse Dance of the Sioux), which won the Grand Purchase Award at Tulsa in 1962, is alive with action and kaleidoscopic color, yet thoroughly Indian in both quality and theme. (See Figure L.)

Blackbear Bosin, a Kiowa-Comanche, won the coveted Special Award at Tulsa in 1967. Earlier he had won a scholarship to the University of Oklahoma and sixteen awards in the annual intertribal competition at the Philbrook Art Center. He has developed a style that accepts the white man's traditional rectangular frame but fills it with decorative figures, which are at home in a natural setting of simplified planes. A recent example of his work, "Of the Owl's Telling," offers a delicately balanced composition that interprets the quiet mysticism of the Plains Indian. (See Figure M.)

The late Oscar Jacobson, who so successfully guided the famed "Kiowa boys" forty years ago, once wrote: "The qualities that endear Indian painting to the art lover are its spontaneous freshness, its subtle simplicity and a marvelous harmony in rhythms and colors that seem to be innate. Indian artists use no models; their keen sense of observation . . . enables them to carry clearly in their minds essential elements of a scene . . . as a result, the Indian's work is direct and powerful."

These qualities continue to be found in the works of present-day Plains Indian artists. Historians of the American West as well as art lovers should be proud that among the descendants of the courageous warriors and big-game hunters of the Great Plains one of America's oldest artistic traditions is still very much alive.

19

HOWLING WOLF

The Life of a Plains Indian

When I hunted the Bufalo I was not poor ...but here I am Poor. I would like to go out on the planes a gain whare I could rome at will and not come back a gain.[1]

So Howling Wolf lamented in 1879, trapped in the poverty of an Indian agency. Four years of prison and reservation life had compelled the young Cheyenne to make the transition from the freedom of a buffalo-hunting nomad-warrior to the confined role defined for him by the white man. Already it was too late to return: in four years both warfare and buffalo herds had vanished from the Southern Plains. Howling Wolf had to content himself with reliving the excitement of the old days with colors and paper. The illustrations that follow constitute his pictorial history and ethnography of the Cheyennes.

In a self-portrait (see p. 45), our artist shows himself in all the glory of a Dance Director for his society, the Bowstring Soldiers. This office was not bestowed lightly; it was accorded to the two bravest men among a membership known for being hot-headed, high-handed, and reckless.

His vaunted bravery is borne out by every glimpse we catch of him as he rides the warpath across the Plains. In May of 1861, at the age of eleven or twelve, Howling Wolf (Honanisto) first went to war—perhaps slipping off with a party enlisted by his father Eagle Head (Minimic), a principal chief of the Cheyennes and a prominent war leader. In 1867 Howling Wolf, now of warrior age, counted his first coup on a raid with a large party of Cheyennes composed chiefly of Bowstring Soldiers. His second coup followed the next year, at Fort Larned, Kansas.[2]

On the Southern Plains, violence now began to increase in tempo until in July, 1874, the United States Army set out to "settle the Indian matter in the Southwest forever." A punishing campaign kept the hostile Cheyennes, Arapahos, Kiowas, and Comanches on the move throughout a winter of great severity. Bereft of horses and tipis, food and clothing, the destitute Indians, a few at a time, trudged into the agency to surrender. But not Howling Wolf. In January it was reported that this "desperate character" was

21

leading a raiding party south to replenish his tribe's supply of horses from the herds at the Wichita Agency or thereabouts "and of course would not hesitate to lift Hair."[3]

In the end all the hostiles had to surrender to the superior power. In April seventy-two warriors from the four tribes started east to be imprisoned as hostages for the good behavior of their people. Some were selected because they were depredators or—like Eagle Head—principal chiefs and ringleaders. Howling Wolf was one of eighteen cut off at random from the end of a line of captives; the first official roster of Cheyennes designated for imprisonment specifies no crime after his name. Instead, the notation reads, "said to have been in favor of peace." On later lists this was changed to read, "Ringleader."[4]

As the doleful party passed through Fort Leavenworth on the way to prison, Eagle Head sought a way out for his son. As one war leader to another, he approached Colonel Nelson A. Miles, recently returned from the campaign against the Cheyennes. Miles later related how the father asked him to take his son "—who was I think one of the handsomest Indians I have ever seen, a stalwart young man of about twenty-two years —and teach him the ways of the white men."[5]

However, it was not Colonel Miles but Lieutenant Richard H. Pratt who was destined to show Howling Wolf the white man's road. When the captives reached their place of imprisonment —the old stone fortress of Fort Marion at St. Augustine, Florida—their jailer, "Captain Pratt," as he was called, set about with compassion and firmness to prepare them for the new life they would find upon release. He provided them with opportunities to work for pay (Howling Wolf drew pictures and on one occasion sent $6.00 to his wife and a friend), to study the three R's (Howling Wolf learned to write and speak Eng-

lish), to join a uniformed military company (at the outset Howling Wolf was a sergeant), and to make friends with the sightseers who thronged the fort.[6]

It was some of the sympathetic visitors, among them the wife of politician George H. Pendleton, of Ohio, who came to the aid of Howling Wolf when his vision began to fail before a year was out at Fort Marion. When Alice Key Pendleton, daughter of Francis Scott Key, returned to her Cincinnati home after a winter holiday in St. Augustine, she obtained the permission of the military authorities to send Howling Wolf to an eminent ophthalmologist, Dr. Cornelius R. Agnew, of New York City, in preference to having a cataract operation performed in St. Augustine at the hands of the post surgeon, Dr. John H. Janeway. By the time the trip materialized, over a year later, there had been a change in plans. Howling Wolf went "to Boston, Mass., in charge of benevolent persons, for treatment to prevent blindness, without expense to the U. S." His travel costs were shared by Mrs. Pendleton and another benefactor ($15.00 apiece), while his expenses for treatment, hospitalization, and five months' stay in Boston were borne by philanthropists there.[7]

His companion on the ocean voyage north in mid-July of 1877 was Lieutenant Edmund L. Zalinski, who was going from St. Francis Barracks, St. Augustine, to Boston to be married. En route, Howling Wolf sent his father a pictographic account of his voyage that, curiously, has come to rest in the collections of a library in Boston. Captain Pratt has recorded the story of the Indian's dramatic return to Fort Marion in December, four months before the prisoners' release:

My house fronted the bay, and persons going to and from the fort generally passed along the sea wall in front of us. We saw a dapper gentleman, with hand satchel, derby hat and cane pass up the sea wall into the fort with quick step, and I went to the fort to see who it was, and found that Howling Wolf had returned unannounced, his eyes greatly benefited, and, in addition, in his dress, manner and conduct, he had imbibed a large stock of Boston qualities; in fact, I was not long in finding out that, in some respects, he had taken on altogether too much Boston for his resources and future good. He became insubordinate and insurrectionary and I was forced to discipline him.[8]

A writer who visited the fort added, "He returned sporting a pair of blue eye-glasses, with all the airs and graces of a Harvard freshman. So thoroughly Bostonian had he become in his short absence that it would have been hardly surprising to hear him reply to the usual Indian greeting 'How?' with an affected 'Nicely'."[9] The husband of the woman who made this observation was an artist, J. Wells Champney, who drew for **Harper's Weekly** a school scene at the fort showing Howling Wolf (upper right); and in the closing months of the Indians' imprisonment, he painted a portrait of Eagle Head, "clad in some of Mrs. Pratt's collection of Indian war toggery," as the captain wrote. Some of the toggery from the portrait appears in a photograph of the old chief and his son, which probably dates from Champney's visit (lower right). Perhaps Howling Wolf donned the costume again when he took part in an "Evening with Mother Goose" talent show. He and a Kiowa named Zotom were billed as "Indians in full war dress, dancing and singing their War song to music of Tomtoms."[10]

The entertainment was staged to raise money for prisoners who wished to remain in the East for further education. Although Pratt had reported Howling Wolf's vision to be improved, the treatment in Boston had not been a complete success. His eyesight prevented his inclusion in the group staying on for school, and sixteen years later he was spoken of as "one-eyed." When the time came for farewells to his venerable

School scene at Fort Marion: Howling Wolf, in glasses, is seated at the far left.

Eagle Head and Howling Wolf, ca. 1877.
(Photo Courtesy of the St. Augustine Historical Society.)

teacher, he displayed a sensibility gratifying to his Victorian friends: " 'Howling Wolf' revealed a lamb couchant somewhere in his nature, as clasping his kind teacher's hand he sobbed, 'Good bye, Miss Mather. Me love you—me love you'."[11]

In May, 1878, Howling Wolf, established at his agency in Darlington, Indian Territory, was traveling the new road he had learned in the East. As soon as he had met Agent John D. Miles en route to the reservation on April 18, Howling Wolf had applied for a position in the agency school. Miles referred the request to the school contractor, John H. Seger. Within a month the agent reported to Pratt that Seger had installed the Indian, his wife, and their four-year-old child in the school:

He as Butcher, moderator [disciplinarian?], and general assistant at a salary (paid by Seger) of $15 per mo. to which I add $5, amt. authorized to be paid to Police.— his wife is being instructed in general house work. They occupy a nice room in the building and take great pride in keeping it in "apple pie" order and that you may know the positive influence exerted by "Howling Wolf" it is my pleasure to inform you that his wife and child have thrown away the Squaw dress and Blanket and have come out boldly on the side of reform.[12]

Still in his first month at the agency, Howling Wolf spoke at a Bible school on the religious training at Fort Marion, and made a prayer— "the first prayer that any present had heard from these Southwestern Indians in their school or meeting." Lawrie Tatum, the former Kiowa agent, while on a visit to the Cheyennes questioned Howling Wolf in an effort to ascertain his religious experience. The Indian's comments reveal his propensity for leadership and give us some insight into his ambitions and philosophy —suggesting that he endorsed the white man's way more in precept than in practice:

I did not think it wrong to raid and fight, which I now believe to be wrong; for I was an Indian, and I thought and acted as an Indian. I wanted to be a leader, and went on in sin, for which I was taken a prisoner, and with others sent to St. Augustine. . . .

I threw away my old road and took the road of the Bible. . . . Now I am holding on to the good road. Since coming here to the school to work, I talk to the boys and girls, urging them to take the good Bible road. . . . I urge all the Indians, Cheyennes and Arapahos, to take the Bible road that they may also be happy.[13]

That same month Howling Wolf made the great coup of his brief life on the new road. He was instrumental in persuading twenty-one men to cut off their scalp locks, put on white man's clothing, and go to work felling trees and making preparations for farming. The event was widely publicized; when the daily press carried the news in July, the number of converts had grown to seventy. Howling Wolf took full credit for the conversions, but Eagle Head called them a joint effort of father and son. The old chief was the head of a band over whom he wielded strong influence. He told Pratt in 1880: "For two winters I have been chopping wood. This is the road the Agent gave me—He said it would be better for me than to raise corn. I have chopped wood for the soldiers and am now chopping for the Agent—and all my people—30 lodges—are working with me." His band cut, sawed, split, stacked, and hauled 2,400 cords a year at $1.25 a cord.[14]

Later events suggest that even in 1878 Howling Wolf aspired to leadership of his father's band. He was nearly thirty, past the age of Cheyenne young-manhood. He had a position of authority in the school; his imprisonment made him a martyr-hero of the late war; he had the advantages of a Fort Marion education; he had established a family. Before he went to prison, he had been married three times and divorced from two wives—Bear Woman and Magpie Woman—by whom he had no issue that lived to maturity. The third wife, Curly Hair (Mamakiaeh), had borne him two daughters and was now following him on the new road. He had firm allies among the young men; his twenty-year-old brother, Little Creek, and his old "friend in raids," Wolf Robe, were among his converts. In the Cheyenne government-by-consensus, a chief was chief only so long as he carried with him the majority of his people. Howling Wolf, by establishing himself as the leader who set his people's feet upon the new road, might immeasurably enhance his prestige.[15]

In December he wrote to his shipmate of the year before, Lieutenant Zalinski. His remarks on the Northern Cheyennes who had slipped away from Darlington to begin the epic trek led by Dull Knife to their home are of particular interest. They effectively confute the allegations made in a recent popular account that Howling Wolf, because he had learned to understand English in Fort Marion, accompanied the northerners to eavesdrop on the pursuing soldiers. While a certain Howling Wolf was indeed fighting his way with Dull Knife, our Howling Wolf was complaining to Zalinski, "I am very poor, as the Northern Cheyennes stole every one of my horses when they left this place last September. When I get some more ponies I shall feel better." He also tells of persuading many men to go to work, of traveling the good road himself (he does not particularize, however), and of trying to induce the Cheyennes to do the same. He has placed his daughter in school and wants the agent to help him build a wooden house to replace his tipi. He hints that some concrete evidence that his friends in the East had not forgotten him would be acceptable.[16]

His career as butcher, moderator, and general assistant in the Cheyenne school ended in February, 1879. Miles spared no effort to provide work, however small the pay, for the returnees who asked for it. Some were agency police, freight haulers, brick moulders; others were rail splitters, hay makers, mail carriers, or, like the old chief Eagle Head and his band, hewers and haulers of wood. Howling Wolf chose to be a farmer. In April, with fifteen other Cheyennes who had finished planting their corn, he was granted a pass by the agent for the rare treat of a two-week visit off the reservation. This marked the end of his first year on the new road. The acting Cheyenne agent described the group as "among the very best disposed Indians on this reserve, whose loyalty has been tried and not found wanting." They perforce conversed in sign language with their hosts, the Poncas and the Pawnees. The Ponca agent called their behavior excellent, but the Pawnee agent believed they were trying to create dissatisfaction among his charges. However, he commended Howling Wolf for giving an encouraging and interesting talk to the school children.[17]

It was at this point that Howling Wolf dictated the letter addressed to Pratt, with which we began. It is so pitilessly self-revealing that it deserves extensive quotation (punctuation and emphasis added). His talk was strong for the white man's road, but his heart still turned to the untrammeled plains:

You gave me the white man's road and it is very good. At the fort you gave us cloths but we have bin here one year and they are about all gon. . . . When I hunted the Bufalo I was not poor; when I was with you I did not want for eney thing but here I am Poor. I would like to go out on the planes a gain whare I could rome at will and not come back a gain. . . . I think thare is a grate meney wild horse in mexico, and if I should goe thare I could capture a hurd and bring them back hear; then I would not be poor. . . . Bare shield, Manimak, Little Medison, and my self have no wagon. I would like to have you talk to Washiton and find out why those tha[t] ware white man's cloths do not get wagons first. The Solder chief plowed my field for me. That made my hart feal good and caused me to recomend the White man's road to the Indin. . . . *My Father is cutting wood while I am looking at my corn.* . . . The White man that has the school in charge is like my Brother. Tomorrow I will kill my Beaf, then will call the cheafs in to my lodg and have a talk and made a road. I think the Trader does not doe right as we don't get as much for five cents as I did in the states.[18]

The white follower of the phonetic system to whom Howling Wolf dictated gave Pratt another view of the Indian, by way of a footnote: "P O He was bound I should write for him. I have done so as he has given it to me. The troubel is he don't like to work but wants to make his living talking." But making a living talking offered a better prospect than farming. In 1879 and again in 1881 a drought all but destroyed the corn crop and discouraged both the Indians and the resourceful agent, who recommended a change from corn to cattle.[19]

This is the last report that presents Howling Wolf as an enthusiastic advocate of the white man's road.

In 1881, the census taker drew a picture of Howling Wolf with a few terse facts: he lived in a cloth lodge, he had worn citizen's dress for five years, he spoke Spanish as well as his native language, he owned one horse, one dog, and a breech-loading rifle. For three years he had cultivated three acres of land. His family consisted of a wife named Curly Head, a son, four little daughters, and a brother, River (also known as Little Creek and Running Water). He gave his occupation as "freighter" (that spring he was attempting to buy his own wagon by hauling freight for the agent).[20]

On May 16 of that year Eagle Head died while laboring to complete a third year's wood contract. While he remained steadfastly on the new road, his son was finding his way back to the road of his forefathers. By mid-1881, only three years after his release from Fort Marion, Howling Wolf was again living much like the corn-growing ancestors he depicted in one of his drawings (see Plate Three, page 43).

His father's death marked a turning point for Howling Wolf. In the fall Agent Miles said, "Howling Wolf, after promising well for a short time after his return, relapsed into his former ways, and is to-day as uncivilized, but not as hostile, as he ever was." On July 10, 1882, Captain Pratt's son Mason reported from Darlington, "I also met Howling Wolf, who dresses as an Indian and is just as much an one as any of them, he has forgotten all his English, does nothing."[21]

Two years later, Howling Wolf became chief of the element the white man called "dog soldiers." In the warlike days before 1875 this term was applied by the whites to the complex of soldier societies of the Plains, doubtless owing to a misapprehension arising from the fame and the ubiquity of the Dog Soldiers, one of the military clubs. Among the Cheyennes, the functions of the old soldier-societies were threefold: civic, military, and social. Howling Wolf's participation in the social and military life of his society, the Bowstrings, has already been mentioned. During June, 1874, when the final revolt against the white oppressor was smoldering in the remote Cheyenne camps, fanned by the promises of the Comanche Isatai, it had been the civil police power of the Bowstring Soldiers that had restrained the peaceful minority from returning to the agency. The Bowstring Soldiers employed the customary expedient of shooting the dissidents' horses and cutting up their lodges, thereby immobilizing them.[22]

Even when the exploits of war had dwindled to oft-recounted coups, the societies persisted. At least some of their civic functions were delegated by Agent Miles to an Indian police force he created when the Fort Marion prisoners returned in 1878. Eleven of the fifteen "Florida Boys" joined the force in May, the month that Howling Wolf went to work at the school. The police were authorized to settle differences and difficulties between individuals and bands, maintain order, settle "pony questions," and prevent trouble in general. Yet when it came to a crisis—when an Indian demanding back-rations coerced the agent into giving them—it was not the "agent's soldiers" but the tribe's "soldier element" that averted a massacre of the whites at the agency by delivering the culprit for punishment.

In April, 1884—the month in which the widely respected Miles was succeeded as agent by "Colonel" D. B. Dyer—Big Man, the chief of the "dog soldiers," died. Howling Wolf succeeded to the chieftaincy of the group. This faction rapidly forced the intransigent Dyer to surrender control of the agency. In emergencies, he found, he could not depend on his police to take action against their own people. He wrote, "My hands are manacled and the dog soldiers rule supreme." Instead of settling down to farming, as he was convinced they should, they were levying tolls on any white man who drove cattle herds or freight trains through their reservation. Besides, he complained, "Why a few score of young bucks should be allowed to . . . compel the attendance of their own people upon the occasion of the medicine-making, whether they believe in it or not, under penalty of having their tents cut up, their dogs, horses, cattle, chickens, etc., killed, and create a disturbance at will, is more than a law-abiding citizen can understand."[23] Clearly, the law-abiding agent did not understand the operation of a long-established Cheyenne law: that the policing of the Sun Dance, the great religious ceremony that yearly drew the scattered members of the tribe together, should be the responsibility of the soldier societies.

In 1885 the leasing of surplus lands to cattlemen had created a pandemonium that could be quieted only by the replacement of Dyer and by the resolute presence of that veteran of the Indian wars, General P. H. Sheridan. He found that "the dog soldiers were saucy and sulky toward the agent," and he interviewed seven representative Cheyenne lease-signers, including Howling Wolf. "They had become sick of the bargain" that gave the ever-encroaching cattlemen the use of nine-tenths of the reservation—about 3,500,000 acres—at a rent of two cents an acre. Upon Sheridan's recommendation to the President, the cattlemen were at once ordered off the reservation. The enlistment of 120 of the restless young men as Army scouts and the appointment of an Army man as agent brought a semblance of peace to the troubled agency. Within a year the agent, Captain J. M. Lee, reported that he had persuaded the Cheyennes to stop their tribal soldiers from exacting attendance at the Sun Dance, and, he added, "being left to their own free will many Indians did not attend." Of the Indian scouts he said, "Instead of being termed 'dog soldiers' for the tribes they are soldiers of the Government."[24]

For a few years thereafter nothing was heard of the "dog soldiers," but a new source of unrest had meanwhile appeared: the question of allotting land to individual Indians and opening the greater part of the reservation to white settlement. Among the Cheyennes, opposition to allotment was strong from the first. Around the elder chief, Stone Calf, in the western part of the reservation, had gathered a group of conservatives who consistently opposed innovation. In 1885 Dyer had called them outlaws who cherished "a bitter hatred for the whites, . . . implacable in their resentment of what they term getting on the white man's road. . . . Their only real grievance is that they do not want to be civilized." Lee had sought to understand them: "These bands are more firmly attached to their old ways and customs, are more spirited in their opposition to what they deem the encroachment of white men." Sheridan interpreted them as a response to the white man's attempt to force acculturation upon a nation determined to preserve the customs and traditions of their fathers. "The Cheyennes are a fine specimen of the wild Indian, and as they still maintain most of their aboriginal customs and a loyalty to the nomadic habits of the uncivilized, nothing could have been more mistaken than an endeavor to crowd upon them in quick succession the customs of civilization."[25]

Thus some ten years after reaching the reservation, Howling Wolf had come full circle. He attached himself to the faction antagonistic to the white man's road, becoming one of its leaders by 1889, after the death of Stone Calf. Agent Charles F. Ashley alleged, among many charges, that this large group of "essentially the non-progressive Indians," were "turbulent, untractable, worthless; they will not listen to reason, and pay but little attention to advice given them by the agent." When the commission negotiating for an allotment agreement in October, 1890, could not concur with the whirlwind opposition on a meeting place, the commission went ahead without the dissidents, "which action ended negotiations so far as this element was concerned." By the use of equally questionable tactics, the allotment agreement was signed and approved by 1891. When the agent began an enrollment preparatory to making cash payments of $75 to each Indian, the opposition refused enrollment, money, or allotments until threatened with loss of their annuities and rations. Allotment was accomplished, said Ashley, despite "the deter-

mined efforts of the wild Indians of the western part of the reservation to defeat it." Each Indian on the reservation got 160 acres, and the tribe received $1,500,000 for about 3,000,000 acres—50 cents an acre.

In May, 1892, Howling Wolf, allottee No. 2102, was assigned his 160 acres of land.[26] In the same year the "red man's Moses," Captain Pratt, spoke out against him publicly in Denver: "Since his return home he has been persistently demanding that he be considered a great man, and has pestered the situation not a little by his assumed superiority."[27]

The following spring Howling Wolf reached the nadir of his turbulent career. He was arrested and indicted for assault on a fourteen-year-old white girl, who was riding horseback on a country road near Watonga, Blaine County, on April 13, 1893. In the jail at Watonga, it was said, "he confessed his crime and gave as an excuse that the white men did that way with the squaws." A deputy sheriff hurried him by night to the jail at Kingfisher, amid rumors that a lynching party would relieve the officer of his prisoner in the canyons east of Watonga. Early in the fall, while awaiting trial, Howling Wolf was moved to El Reno, Canadian County, and there broke jail. He was reported in October to have appeared at an Indian dance in his old Blaine County haunts. "He said that the moon is now all covered over with blood and that some of the pale faces in this vicinity will start for the Blessed Prairie just as soon as he can get at them."

In January, as though enacting a conventional Western, the Canadian County sheriff and a posse of deputies were chasing the bad Indian across the plains of Blaine County, some sixty or seventy miles from the agency. They closed in on him just as he ran into an Indian camp, but here his people failed to follow the script. "When he was found he was surrounded by a

By the end of his life, Howling Wolf had returned to the ways of an Indian—with certain changes. While at a Sun Dance ceremony in 1913, he was painted carrying the symbols—gourd and feathers—of the new Cheyenne religion: the Native American Church, which combined elements of Christianity with the use of the hallucinogenic drug peyote. Coy Avon Seward, a white artist, sought out Howling Wolf at the Sun Dance camp and asked to take his photograph. "The old man," reported Seward, "would not let me take a photo but said I could 'write' his picture if I wanted to."
(Portrait courtesy of the Kansas State Historical Society.)

band of 200 warriors who refused to give him up and laughed in the face of the officer. He had to return without Mr. Howling Wolf or fight the entire band, and so he retired." "The officers increased their force and declare that they will take him dead or alive."[28]

With this exciting episode, the sponsors dropped the serial. Indeed, the local authorities dropped the affair into the lap of the Indian agent. This harried man, pleading insufficient resources, attempted to pass it to the military. Washington, understandably loathe to risk another Battle of Wounded Knee, tried, by means of some deft legalistic juggling, to turn responsibility back to the civil authorities of the Territory of Oklahoma. During this offstage bickering, the villain of the piece dropped out of sight. "For seven or eight years he was a fugitive from justice, hiding among the Kiowa and Comanche. When charges against him were dismissed he returned to his home near Kingfisher."[29]

We read of another confrontation of Howling Wolf and the white man, this one at a Baptist camp meeting on Kingfisher Creek in 1911:

The last service is now under way. It is Sunday afternoon and the Indian women and girls have donned all their finery. The tent is a blaze of color and everywhere is the fragrance of the Indian perfume, "wah-wah-shawn," or "sweet-smelling leaves," which the Arapahoe find along the South Canadian. . . .

The wife and small son of Howling Wolf, the Cheyenne, have come forward. Howling Wolf himself stands in the background. He has been a bad Indian; one of the worst on the warpath, and showing little improvement in later years. . . .

In the last year or two there has been a change in Howling Wolf, and he has talked of becoming a Christian, weary of the "crooked road." To the surprise of both the missionaries and of the Indians, Howling Wolf advances and stops a few feet back of the chair in which his wife is sitting. There he stands irresolute, torn with conflicting emotions and scanned by every eye. For half an hour this Indian stood there and fought a great battle with his heart and his conscience. King, the Arapahoe missionary,

expert in the use of the sign language, caught the attention of Howling Wolf, and with his hands and fingers besought the old man to turn to the "Jesus road." Howling Wolf intently watched every movement, nodding his head at intervals.

Then came disaster. It was not learned whether Howling Wolf intended to approach his wife to speak to her or to sit beside her, but as he stepped forward the Christian Kiowa and Comanche, who knew the manner of life he had led, suddenly began exclaiming, "A-ho! A-ho! A-ho!" meaning, "It is good, it is well," etc. Howling Wolf faltered and then fled. His courage failed him at the last moment.[30]

IN 1927 HOWLING WOLF, aged 77, was living at Cantonment, Oklahoma, the stronghold of conservatism among the Southern Cheyennes. His wife had died, and in May the "Chief" left for Texas with his son Jonathan and Jonathan's wife and baby. Howling Wolf was to re-create his youthful days by setting up an Indian village in the municipal park at Houston and dancing twice a day for four months—on a salary. The Indians' manager, a W. R. Block, was quoted as saying he was taking no Indians to Houston except those of high standing and none that used liquor. In August, Jonathan testified:

My father, William Shore, and I started from Houston Texas for Cantonment Agency, Oklahoma about July 1st. and when we were about seventeen miles from Waurika [Oklahoma] another car . . . hit our car and caused us to hit a culvert and our car turned entirely over into a deep ditch. The car that hit us never did stop and we do not know who did it or whose car it was. We got help and after finding that Howling Wolf was badly hurt, got him taken to the hospital at Waurika, where he died the next day.[31]

Howling Wolf's life had spanned the transitional years between the era of the equestrian nomad shown in his drawings and the age of the automobile, which was instrumental in his death. Yet he died as he had lived, striving to recapture the way of life of his youth.

THE PLATES

On the following pages are reproduced the twelve colorful scenes from *Howling Wolf's* sketchbook.

The artist worked in a commercially-produced drawing pad, outlining his figures in ink, then filling in with color. The fill is usually watercolor, but occasionally ink (as for the buffalo in Plates One and Seven) or an opaque tempera-like paint (as for the squash in Plate Three). Curiously, a sizing has been applied to the green areas of Plate Eight—recalling a technique long used by Plains Indians for painting buffalo hides.

The italic captions for each plate are taken from the original sketchbook, where they were written in the hand of Ben Clark, a scout and post interpreter at Fort Reno during the years Howling Wolf was living at the agency nearby. These captions indicate that the drawings were executed sometime between 1878 and 1881, making them the only known sketchbook by a Cheyenne from Fort Marion after his return home.

Ben Clark was "a man of clear intellect, expressing himself in good language, honest and truthful in his statements and accurate in his deductions," according to Lieutenant (later Captain) John G. Bourke, then aide-de-camp to General George Crooke, commanding officer of the Department of the Platte. In 1878 campaigns against the Indians brought Bourke and Clark together frequently, and the two men had long discussions about the culture and history of the Cheyennes. Clark apparently entrusted the Howling Wolf sketchbook to Bourke—a fortunate choice, for Captain Bourke later became eminent as an ethnologist, and it is through his efforts that the drawings have been preserved.

The sketchbook is now in the possession of Captain Bourke's daughter, Mrs. A. H. (Anna Bourke) Richardson, and was on loan to the Joslyn Art Museum, Omaha, at the time these plates were made.

PLATE ONE:
THE FIRST WHITE MAN

The first White men seen by the Cheyennes, over 100 yrs ago on the Missouri River above the mouth of the Cheyenne River in a Sioux Camp. White men came from the northwest according to their tradition. Cheyennes with dog travois on right.

The event commemorated here was destined first to produce the flowering of Cheyenne culture and then to bring about the end of the Indians' way of life. In the central group of figures, a white man strides forward (identified by his tight, plain clothing, the holster on his hip, and heels on his shoes) to grasp the hand of the Cheyenne leader of a trading party. Behind the white man the Sioux chief steps out from the side of his wife and baby (as his foot tracks show). His extended pipe is both the symbol of his rank and the sign of friendly intent toward the Cheyennes. To his rear, a blanket-wrapped crier flourishes a bird-wing fan as he summons the people for a session of trading.

Neither tribe as yet owns horses; even the chief resorts to a dog for transportation. The animal that he leads toward the trading party is already harnessed to receive a pack of goods. The arrival of the Cheyennes to trade, then, was anticipated in the Sioux camp.

PLATE ONE:

Indeed, the Sioux probably sent runners to the Cheyenne camp with news of the arrival of white traders, for the Cheyenne leader was obviously prepared. Foreknowledge would account for two things: first, the symbolic gun, indicating the kind of trade the leader has in mind, in contrast to the bows and arrows conspicuously displayed by his party to show that these were their only weapons; second, the forthrightness and aplomb — not to say cordiality — with which the Cheyenne meets the exotic stranger. His eagerness to meet the white man at first hand is understandable; here is the source of many of the good things of life — guns, knives, axes, kettles, bits of steel, and beads.

Prospects for trading are bright — the white traders have camped with the Sioux. The man in the foreground has unhitched the mule, tethered the horse, unloaded some of the packs of trade goods, pitched the canvas tent, and is now cooking a meal, while a comrade, in coonskin cap, looks on. The Cheyennes have come prepared. Their dog-travois are loaded, presumably with dried meat or tanned hides.

At the top of the picture, which conventionally indicates distance away, the women of the Cheyenne buffalo-hunting camp are laboring to produce more staples for trade or home consumption. They are drying slabs of meat in the sun on racks and tanning hides stretched on a frame or pegged to the ground. Their camp is strategically located near a place where the buffalo come down to the Missouri to drink.

This drawing illustrates the difference between the white man's written history and Indian tradition. The former records the first contact with the Cheyennes (by LaSalle) in 1680 in what is now Illinois, a milieu of canoe and waterway, forest and longhouse, beaver and deer. It further relates that before the white men saw them again, the Cheyennes moved

36

PLATE ONE:

from the upper Mississippi and Minnesota rivers in what is now Minnesota to the Sheyenne River in southeastern North Dakota. Here they were visited by neither white travelers nor traders. Their contact with the white man increased but little when, after 1750, they gradually moved to the earth-lodge villages of the Plains, near the point at which the Missouri River crosses into present-day South Dakota. Here they met the Sioux, with whom they were alternately at peace and at war. At the end of the century, when they abandoned Village-Dweller life, white traders were still a novelty to the Cheyennes.

At the time this picture was painted, about 1880, memories of the Cheyennes' Woodland Era had grown dim. The meeting with the white man in 1680, seven hundred miles to the east of this scene, had dropped out of Cheyenne tradition. Instead, the encounter is pictured as taking place on the Plains. The absence of horses among these Cheyennes shows that they had not yet become equestrian nomads. A hunting trip on foot to the mouth of the Cheyenne River in central South Dakota suggests that the permanent village of the Cheyennes was now on the Missouri rather than the Sheyenne. The event's date was therefore in the second half of the eighteenth century, according to white man's history. Contact with the trader would probably have occurred soon after the Indians moved out of their Sheyenne River isolation to the village crossroads of trade, both intertribal and Indian-white. Howling Wolf, the Indian artist, agrees by placing the scene before 1780. If this drawing is considered as depicting the first white contact on the Plains, it is a generally accurate rendition, although it should be noted that the wagon in the lower left of the picture was an exercise in imagination; traders on the Upper Missouri in the eighteenth century did not use wagons.

PLATE TWO:
THE FIRST HORSES

The first horses owned by Cheyennes which they are trading for from the Kiowas on the Arkansas or what the Indians call Flint River the arrow indicating the name from its flint head. Supposed to be over 150 yrs ago. Cheyennes on right with dog travois, Kiowas on left.

This significant drawing had been removed from the book seventy years ago and had disappeared. The author found it on a research trip in 1966, and it has now been restored to its place in the drawing book.

The coming of the horse revolutionized the entire way of life of the Plains Indian. Hence, the event was a high point in any tribe's history. Because the horse and the gun were equally prized, the custom arose that when a horse was offered in trade, it was paid for with a gun, powder, or musket balls; and vice versa. The Cheyenne at the right in the center foreground clasps hands in friendship with Satank, or Sitting Bear, the great man of the Kiowas. Sitting Bear is identified by the name-symbol connected to his head. He leads a horse obtained from the white man, as the brand reveals. His intent is to trade it for the pack

to which the Cheyenne is pointing, carried on the dog-travois. The pack's compact size suggests musket balls. A second Cheyenne customer waits behind the dog, holding out a powder horn that he wants to trade. Another, with a gun, lurks in the background, concealed by hillock and tree.

Another transaction has already taken place, represented by the **X** symbol that signifies exchange. A Kiowa, to obtain the rifle that he is now embracing, had led his horse out from the Kiowa camp toward the Cheyennes, as the hoofprints show. When the exchange was accomplished, the Cheyenne chief in the foreground, identified by the pipe-tomahawk, called forth his wife to take charge of the horse. Her sex is indicated by her plain leggings and the dress with fringed side-panels. Her footsteps tell that she led away the skittish "giant dog." An old hand at intimidating the pack-dogs, she nevertheless keeps a safe distance as she turns and addresses a few remarks to her charge (as the lines from her mouth suggest).

Another famous Kiowa, Satanta or White Bear, has also come to trade. Before his tipi, at the upper left, stand his wife and his personal medicine-lance or zebo, made in the form of a giant red-feathered arrow. Oblivious to all the ceremony, a small boy lies on his back on the river bank and practices marksmanship on a bird in the treetop. The stone tip of the arrow at the top of the picture is connected by a line to its namesake, the Flint River, called by the white man the Arkansas.

White historians say of the acquisition of the horse by the Cheyennes: In present North Dakota, the Cheyennes lived a typical semi-sedentary Village-Dweller life in great earth lodges and practiced horticulture. Here, about 1750, they began to acquire horses and with their help came to depend increasingly on the buffalo for subsistence. Apparently they did not have the gun here but hunted with bow and arrow, and lance.

In dating this event as about 1730, Cheyenne tradition differs by only some twenty years from the white man's date, but it places the occurrence some six hundred or seven hundred miles to the south, in a buffalo-culture setting of tipi camps on the Arkansas, where the Cheyennes are well supplied with guns and ammunition. The artist-historian has substituted a more recent and familiar locale for that of the nearly forgotten past.

HORTICULTURE

C*heyenne corn field of the olden time. Their Tradition has it that up to about 200 years ago or more, before they had crossed to the south or west side of the Missouri River they raised corn, supposed they lived well up towards British America probably on the Red River of the North. The Ree's occupied their corn patches after they left.*

Howling Wolf is not suggesting that the prodigious Cheyenne squash grew on trees. Rather, he is using the usual Plains artistic convention for distance: the farther away the object, the higher in the picture it should be placed.

According to the white man's account, by 1684 the tribe was living in the fertile Minnesota River Valley and presumably was practicing horticulture. By the eighteenth century they had located in earth lodges on the Sheyenne River, near the Red River of the North, and raised corn, squash, and beans to supplement their buffalo-meat diet. So plentiful were their crops that they traded surplus produce with neighboring Chippewas. From this place they migrated west to the Missouri, where at first they lived in the earth-lodge villages, continued their horticulture, and intermarried with their neighbors and allies, the village-dwelling Arikaras (Rees). Thence they moved southwest toward the Black Hills. In 1802, according to one report, they were seasonal nomads who planted corn in the spring and returned in the fall from their wandering hunts to harvest it. Another traveler averred that, by 1804, they had abandoned horticulture and the Village for the life of the nomadic hunter.

The date of the Cheyennes' traditional timetable — 1680 or before — agrees remarkably with the earliest date the white historian assigns them for horticulture on the Minnesota, but would hardly be acceptable as a terminal date. It is too early for the periods when they lived near the Red River (beginning 1700) and close to the Rees (beginning 1750). Indian traditional history telescoped the three sites into one.

Howling Wolf has depicted a typical scene of his day, even showing one of the garden plots in which the artist and many other Cheyennes were striving to raise corn. By her tipi the woman has built an arching brush-shelter as a summer kitchen. Like the figures in the preceding plates, she wears the dress of the 1870's — in this case a choker, cape sleeves, side panels, and silver belt with dropper. In their true horticultural period the Cheyennes did not live in the tipi, except perhaps while hunting. It became their year-round home only when they became nomads with merely haphazard attempts at gardening. Again the artist has filled in for the forgotten details of the past with the known, more recent locale.

W*ar Dance, before departing on War Path. Howling Wolf is on horse back.*

The warlike scenes that follow are laid in the two decades before 1875, the date at which war ended for the Southern Cheyennes. The purpose of the dance pictured here was to drum up enthusiasm and enlist recruits for a raid.

The tribe at this time was divided into five soldier societies, each with its own officers and regalia, songs and dances, customs and ritual. "The societies are not organized trainbands of the order of colonial militia in the early days of American settlement. They are, in their way, somewhat more comparable to local American Legion or V.F.W. posts — social and civic organizations mainly centered on the common experience of the members as warriors, with rituals glorifying and enhancing that experience, and with duties and services performed on behalf of the community at large."[1]

The duties of the soldier societies included such civil functions as regulating the tribal hunts, policing the great ceremonies, organizing the moving of the camp, and consulting with the tribal council on important matters of policy.

The orderly dancing of the societies was directed by the two bravest members. Howling Wolf, identified by his name-symbol, portrays himself as one of those selected for this honorific position by his society, the Bowstring Soldiers. Upon both himself and his horse he has painted the symbol for wounds, to commemorate the perils he has run. Beside their fraternal tipi, the young men of this gayest and noisiest of the societies dance in two opposing lines, jumping up and down in place. The rhythm is set by the four old-men drummers. Behind stand the admiring women.

All eyes are turned to the dancer brandishing the tomahawk. Howling Wolf has honored the eminent warrior by calling him up to close the dance by counting coup, as was the custom of the Bowstrings. The coup-counter narrates, with full pantomime, the story of some of his valiant deeds of battle.

PLATE FIVE:
RETURN OF A WAR PARTY

*W*arriors returning from a Raid Led by war Chief "Roman Nose." They fire their guns and yell as the[y] near the village.

Roman Nose, the great Northern Cheyenne war leader of the Southern Cheyennes, is unmistakably identified here. The protective warbonnet he is wearing brought him safely through two fights in which his horse was shot out from under him, the charge on Colonel Nelson Cole's troops in 1865 and the attack on Custer's supply train in 1867. Here Roman Nose has had another close call; his wounded war-horse still carries the point of an arrow in its flesh. The warrior was to meet his death in 1868 at the fight of Beecher's Island, when the medicine of his famous bonnet was broken.

In a war-based society, it is only natural that Roman Nose should have been a tribal hero:

"The Cheyenne men were all warriors. War was regarded as the noblest of pursuits, the only one for a man to follow; and from earliest youth boys were encouraged to excel in it. They were taught that no pleasure equaled the joy of battle; that success in war brought in its train the respect and admiration of men, women, and children in the tribe, and that the most worthy thing that any man could do was to be brave. It was pointed out that death in battle was not an evil, and that such a death, besides being glorious, protected one from all the miseries which threaten later life and are inevitable to old age."[2]

When a successful returning war party was close enough to their village to hear the dogs barking, they stopped behind a ridge and donned their best war-clothes. They tried to take the camp by surprise, riding quietly until close enough to make a charge. In a line, the war party pictured is charging the village, waving the scalps taken and firing in celebration. Their people hurry out to see the parade, cheering and shouting for the heroes and singing songs of victory. The drawing shows the puffs of smoke and the path of the projectiles. The party has been successful; four scalps wave in the air.

PLATE SIX:
SCALPING

Scalp Dance. Scalps dangling from poles held by squaws, also an arm.

"The general opinion that the act of scalping reflects credit on the warrior has no foundation. The belief perhaps arose from the fact that, when an enemy was killed or wounded, brave Indians rushed toward him. White observers have very likely inferred that those who were rushing upon an enemy were eager to take his scalp. As a matter of fact they cared little or nothing for the scalp but very much for the credit of touching the fallen man....

"Among the plains tribes a scalp was a mere trophy and was not highly valued. It was regarded as an emblem of victory and was a good thing to carry back to the village to rejoice and dance over. But any part of an enemy's body might serve for this, and it was not at all uncommon among the Blackfeet to take off a leg or an arm, or even a foot or hand, to carry back and rejoice over for weeks and months. Very commonly, a party returning from war would give one or more scalps to a group of old men and old women, who would paint their faces black and carry the scalp all about through the village dancing at intervals, singing the praises of the successful warriors, making speeches in their honor, and generally rejoicing.... Scalps were used to trim and fringe war clothing—shirts and leggings—and to tie to the horse's bridle in going to war. Usually the scalps taken were small, a little larger than a silver dollar, but like any other piece of fresh skin they stretched greatly."[3]

Women dominate the scalp dance, a celebration of their men's success in war. The three male singers and drummers are at the left. Two warriors next to them stand ready, when called upon, to recount their brave deeds in the past battle, one demonstrating with a streamered sword. The rest of the dancers are women, identified by their hair-parts and conch belts with droppers. In the center burns the "skunk," so called from the plumed tail of smoke. The dance will probably be repeated for many days to come. Other grim souvenirs are displayed on the tall lodge pole above the tipi at the left—five scalps captured in former battles.

BUFFALO CULTURE

B*uffalo Hunt. If any animal was ever designed by the hand of nature for the express purpose of supplying, at one stroke, nearly all the wants of an entire race, surely the buffalo was intended for the Indian.*

"And right well was this gift of the gods utilized by the children of nature to whom it came....Of the many different uses to which the buffalo and his various parts were put by the red man, the following were the principal ones:

"The body of the buffalo yielded fresh meat, of which thousands of tons were consumed; dried meat, prepared in summer for winter use; pemmican (also prepared in summer) of meat, fat, and berries; tallow, made up into large balls or sacks, and kept in store; marrow, preserved in bladders; and tongues, dried and smoked, and eaten as a delicacy.

"The skin of the buffalo yielded a robe, dressed with the hair on, for clothing and bedding; a hide, dressed without the hair, which made a teepee cover, when a number were sewn together....Shields, made from the thickest portions, as rawhide; ropes, made up as rawhide; clothing of many kinds; bags for use in traveling; coffins, or winding sheets for the dead, etc.

"Other portions utilized were sinews, which furnished fiber for ropes, thread, bow-strings, snow-shoe webs, etc.; hair, which was sometimes made into belts and ornaments; 'buffalo chips,' which formed a valuable and highly prized fuel; bones, from which many articles of use and ornament were made; horns, which were made into spoons, drinking vessels, etc."[4]

In the upper right of the drawing, a horse slips as the hunter closes in for the kill. A buffalo is belligerent when wounded; the man is in imminent danger of being gored.

PLATE EIGHT:
RELIGION

*M*edicine Lodge. Commencement of Ceremony, the grand entry of the Medicine Men, who all shoot at the little image hanging at the Centre Pole.

Called by the white man the Sun Dance, this was a richly symbolic ceremony—the great annual event that unified the scattered tribe. It was put on by one or more men, known as Sun Dance Makers, in fulfillment of a vow in time of trouble.

"The one who vowed a [Sun Dance] ceremony wanted 'life' or 'life power' and removal of whatever was between him and that 'life'. What he vowed was always wished by his next friends, his band and the whole tribe, so the ceremony was to bring the life giving power, to make the sick well and promote reproduction not only among the [Cheyennes] themselves but among the animals and plants upon which they mostly depended."[5]

In this drawing, the members of the soldier society of the Sun Dance Makers are performing the opening ceremony of the Sun Dance proper after four preliminary days. They march in, led by two notable men who are mounted, carrying lances and other weapons, and wearing their warbonnets. One of the riders is seen in profile at the left of the center pole. Just inside the tent eight footmen stand by their lances, facing the center pole. They are firing (as indicated by the seven cone-shaped symbols above) at a dangling rawhide figure representing, by the style of his moccasins, the enemy.

The drummers and singers are in the center foreground. The crowd presses close for a better view. Several carry umbrellas against the heat of the long day. The Sun Dance structure is presented as if seen from above at a 45-degree angle.

PLATE NINE:
HORSE RACING

A n old fashioned horse race, run to a given point and turn and run back to starting point, generally such races are from 2 to 4 miles. (Judges are on knoll with flag.)

As an old Cheyenne related:

"Competitive sports used to interest us. Horse races, foot races, wrestling matches, target shooting with guns or with arrows, tossing the arrows by hand, swimming, jumping and other like contests were entered upon. In the tribe such competition usually was between men representing the three warrior societies.... If any Sioux tribe or big band camped jointly with us the matches were between representative members of the two tribes. Bets were made on every kind of contest. The stakes were of guns, ammunition, bows and arrows, blankets, horses, robes, jewelry, shirts, leggings, moccasins, everything in the line of personal property. The betting always was on even terms. Articles were piled upon a blanket, matched articles in apposition to each other. The winners took all and shouted over the victory."[6]

Indian pictography has the advantage of showing past and present time simultaneously. The starters on a knoll at the upper left corner fire their guns. As the hoofprints show, the racers gallop down to the stream, cross it, then race around the judges' knoll and up to the plain. The painted end of a buffalo scapula, high on a pole, points the direction of the course. The judges are stationed to guard against foul play by the contestants while out of sight of the spectators.

Drawn up in formal lines to await the finish are members of the two competing sides, their lance streamers a-flutter. Between the lines lie the stakes wagered: quiver and light-colored horse versus lance and dark horse; weapons, quiver, and folded robe.

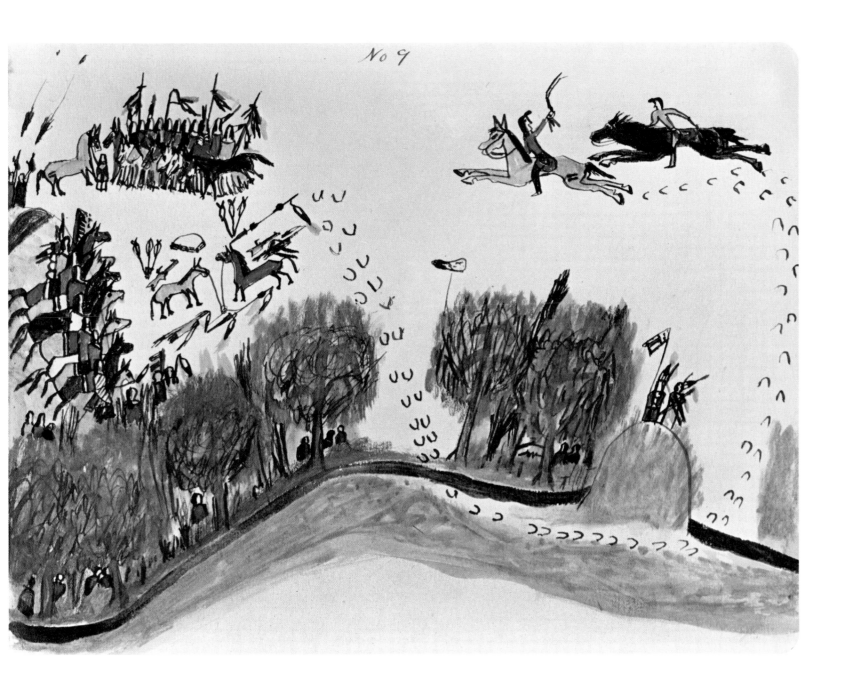

A*young man stealing and eloping with a girl, one way of marriage.*

Ben Clark, who wrote this caption in Howling Wolf's book, obtained the drawings for Captain John G. Bourke and, in the course of a friendship of several years, conveyed to Bourke considerable first-hand information on Cheyenne customs, which Bourke recorded. The following excerpt from Bourke's diary could thus be considered an enlargement by Clark on his brief caption. In telling of courtship customs, he says that the first step is for the suitor formally to make his intentions known to the girl.

"The lover now has to wait until he can catch the young maiden coming out of her lodge, when he will seize her in his arms and wrap his blanket about her. This is a formal declaration of his love.... When the young lady's heart has been won, the suitor must apply for her hand, not to her parents but to her 'guardian', who is most frequently an older brother, altho' he may be some other relative. This wardship is an odd feature. The mother and father probably exercise great influence in the matter, but externally at least, the guardian has full powers: these, he may exercise arbitrarily, and in that case the young lady, to escape a marriage repugnant to her notions, often will elope with the favored lover."'

An elopement was not the socially accepted method of marriage, and was seldom practiced among the Cheyennes. The father or brother of the girl had the right to pursue the couple and bring the girl back home.

Here the maiden named Arrow has come out of her home, one of the Cheyennes' rare painted tipis with heraldic designs (the home of Red Cloud). As the many footprints show, she has talked for some time with her suitor (who may be named Sharp Nose). He starts to lead her away; she hesitates and then capitulates.

Both lovers are dressed in the ultimate of Cheyenne finery. The man: dentalium-shell earring, wrapped braids, calico shirt, silver armbands, vest, breastplate with dangling silver ornament, bandolier, hairplates, robe with wide embroidered strip, and sword with otterskin streamers with feathers. The girl: dentalium earrings, elk-tooth dress, hairpipe necklace, concho belt with dropper, belt-bag, skirt with side panel, bracelets, and fringed blanket.

No. 10

PLATE ELEVEN: SOCIAL DANCING

Sociable Dance, young men and women dancing for pleasure.

As with Plate 10, Captain Bourke has quoted Ben Clark :

"They take great pleasure in the dance and will organize parties for that purpose upon the slightest pretext. In one of these, the participants take their place in couples; while dancing, the young buck will sing to the girl who happens to be his partner—'I am looking for a nice girl to live with me and be my wife and stay with me wherever I go; I think I see the girl I am looking for'. The young lady answers in the same strain and then they join hands and dance together down the line'."[8]

In this picture, the man, facing the girl, wraps his blanket around her. The orchestra at the left pounds on a drum that is not the individual hand instrument of the soldier-society dance nor a shapeless piece of rawhide as in the Sun Dance, but is similar to a bass drum in appearance—an innovation for the Cheyennes. The sides of the tipi are rolled up to provide ventilation and to give the spectators at the right a better view.

Antelope Hunt. Most civilized writers seem to have assumed that hunting was all pleasure. This view is taken because to the white man hunting is a pastime, a recreation, and we assume that it is so to all people.…To the Plains Indian hunting was never a recreation, but was the chief labor by which he supported life.

"Writers, quite ignorant of Indians, but who wish to give local color to fanciful descriptions of Indian hunting, sometimes describe the hunters as yelling in the excitement of the chase. It would be as fitting to write of a farmer as yelling in the excitement of plowing or of milking his cows."[9]

The "antelope" in the foreground are, strictly speaking, pronghorns (identified by the horns and the bands on the breast). They are exceedingly fleet little animals, and only the horse selected for his speed could overtake them. In the distance, a spotted dog chases a deer, which the wagging tail indicates is a white-tail.

Curiously, the hunters are equipped as if for war. The farthest horse wears his medicine paint (seen in contrast to the conventionalized spots of the dog). Every man carries his sacred shield—hardly a fitting article to take on a hunt. Perhaps on the way to make a raid the warriors have chanced on a herd of antelope. Their fast war-horses are equal to the challenge.

FOOTNOTES FOR HOWLING WOLF

1 Howling Wolf to Pratt, June 5, 1879, General Richard H. Pratt Papers, MSS, Western Americana Collection, Beinecke Rare Book and Manuscript Library, Yale University, New Haven, Conn. (hereinafter cited as Pratt Papers).

2 James Mooney, MS 2531, field notebooks, V, pp. 38-38a, Bureau of American Ethnology Collection, Office of Anthropology Archives, Smithsonian Institution, Washington, D.C.; Karen D. Petersen, "Cheyenne Soldier Societies," **Plains Anthropologist,** IX, No. 25 (Aug. 1964), Table 2, 164; Lawrie Tatum, letter, May 15, 1878, **Friends' Review** (n. d.), pp. 667-668; R. H. Pratt, 'Catalogue of Casts Taken by Clark Mills, Esq., of the Heads of Sixty-four Indian Prisoners of Various Western Tribes and Held at Fort Marion, Saint Augustine, Fla., in Charge of Capt. R. H. Pratt, U.S.A.,' "Proceedings of the United States National Museum," 1878, I, **Smithsonian Miscellaneous Collections,** XIX (Washington, D.C., 1880), p. 204; list of Cheyenne Indians held as prisoners at Cheyenne Agency, Ind. Tr., Oklahoma Historical Society, Indian Archives, Oklahoma City, Okla. (hereinafter cited as OHSIA) Cheyenne and Arapaho—Indian Prisoners; George Bird Grinnell, **The Cheyenne Indians** (New York, 1962), Vol. II, p. 196. For the only known picture of the Bowstring Society of this time with the bowed and strung lances from which they take their name, see William Cohoe, **A Cheyenne Sketchbook** (Norman, Okla., 1964), commentary by E. Adamson Hoebel and Karen Daniels Petersen, p. 53, Plate 7.

3 Donald J. Berthrong, **The Southern Cheyennes** (Norman, Okla., 1963), p. 390, quoting Sheridan; Agent Miles to Agent Haworth, Jan. 21, 1875, National Archives, War Department, Record Group 94, Adjutant General's Office (hereinafter cited as NAWD, RG—, AGO), Adjutant General's letters received, File 2815-1874.

4 Agent Miles to Commissioner Smith, Apr. 29, 1875, National Archives, Office of Indian Affairs, Record Group 75 (hereinafter cited as NAOIA, RG—); Pratt, **Smithsonian Miscellaneous Collections,** XIX, p. 204.

5 General Nelson A. Miles, **Personal Recollections** (Chicago, 1897), p. 179.

6 "Catalogue of the Art of the Indians Imprisoned at Fort Marion, Florida, 1875–78," in William Cohoe, **A Cheyenne Sketchbook,** pp. 91–93; Agent Miles to Pratt, Aug. 23, 1876, and drawing book by Making Medicine and others, Pratt Papers; Pratt to Agent Covington, Aug. 14, 1875, OHSIA, Cheyenne and Arapaho—Indian Prisoners. Two additional sketchbooks by Howling Wolf from Fort Marion have come to light since publication of the "Catalogue of Art" cited above. Eight drawings signed jointly with Soaring Eagle are in the Field Museum of Natural History, Chicago. Sixteen are with the Western Americana Collection of the Beinecke Rare Book and Manuscript Library at Yale University. From the latter set, a recent book reproduces a hunting scene, erroneously identifying Howling Wolf as a Northern, instead of a Southern, Cheyenne. John Stands In Timber and Margot Liberty with Robert M. Utley, **Cheyenne Memories** (New Haven, Conn., 1967), facing p. 52.

7 Mary Selden Kennedy, **The Seldens of Virginia** (New York, 1911), p. 188; Alice Key Pendleton to Pratt, May 19, 1876, Aug. 14, 1877, Pratt Papers; Lt. R. H. Pratt, Report of Indian Prisoners Confined in Fort Marion, St. Augustine, Florida, during the month of August, 1877, NAOIA RG 75, letters received, Central Superintendency, 1877; Mary D. Burnham, "Cheyennes, Kiowas, and Comanches," **Churchman,** XXXVIII, No. 4 (July 27, 1878), p. 103; Pratt to Mrs. Pendleton, Jan. 6, 1878, Pratt Papers; Pratt, **Address before the National Convention of Charities and Correction at Denver, Colorado, June 28, '92,** p. 2.

8 Selected documents relating to Major Edmund L. Zalinski, 1960, NAWD, RG 94, AGO; picture letter by Howling Wolf, Francis Parkman Papers, Massachusetts Historical Society, Boston; Pratt, **Address before the National Convention,** p. 2.

9 Lizzie W. Champney, "The Indians at San Marco," **Independent,** XXX, No. 1541 (New York, June 13, 1878), p. 27.

10 J. Wells Champney, "Indian School at Fort Marion, St. Augustine, Florida," **Harper's Weekly,** XXII, No. 1115 (May 11, 1878), p. 373; Robert J. McKay, "Biography," **James Wells Champney, 1843–1903** (Deerfield, Mass., 1965), pp. 12, 16; Brig. Gen. Richard Henry Pratt, **Battlefield and Classroom: Four Decades with the American Indian, 1867–1904,** ed. Robert M. Utley (New Haven, Conn., 1964), p. 185; handbill for Mother Goose evening, Mar. 4, 1878, Pratt Papers. Pratt's remarkable memoirs include chapters on the Fort Marion episode.

11 Burnham, **Churchman,** XXXVIII, No. 4, p. 103; "Still at Large," **Daily Herald** (El Reno, Okla.), Feb. 2, 1894, p. 2; Helen W. Ludlow, "The Indian Work at Hampton Institute," **Good Company,** XIV, No. 4 (1879).

12 Agent Miles to Pratt, May 23, 1878, Pratt Papers; for a short biographical note on the dedicated agent John DeBras Miles, see Hubert E. Collins, "Ben Williams, Frontier Peace Officer," **Chronicles of Oklahoma,** X, No. 4 (Dec. 1932), pp. 521–22, n. 2.

13 Lawrie Tatum, letters, May 6, 15, 1878, **Friends' Review** (n. d.), pp. 651, 667–68.

14 Agent Miles to Commissioner Hayt, Report for May, 1878, June 1, 1878. NAOIA, RG 75, Letters Received, Cheyenne and Arapaho, 1878; Burnham, **Churchman,** p. 103; Howling Wolf to Zalinski, Dec. 21, 1878, **Southern Workman,** VIII, No. 2 (Feb. 1879), p. 19; Minimic to Pratt, Oct. 26, 1878, and Mahnimick to Pratt, Jan. 26, 1880, Pratt Papers; Pratt, **Battlefield and Classroom,** p. 165; Minimic to Pratt, Jan. 24, 1879, **Southern Workman,** VIII, No. 3 (March 1879), p. 31.

15 No. 2102, Howling Wolf, allotment file, Cheyenne-Arapaho

Area Field Office, Concho, Okla.; 10th Census of the U.S., Indian Division, Cheyenne Tribe, Mar. 14, 1881, Sheet No. 245, OHSIA, Census; Howling Wolf to Pratt, June 5, 1879 and Miles to Pratt, May 23, 1878, Pratt Papers.

16 Howling Wolf to Zalinski, Dec. 21, 1878, p. 19; Mari Sandoz, **Cheyenne Autumn** (New York, 1953), pp. 33, 52, and **passim;** Miles (to Commissioner), Nov. 15, 1878, NAOIA, RG 75, letters received, Cheyenne and Arapaho, 1878, M2141.

17 Record of Indian Police [1878–1880], NAOIA, RG 75, Statistics Division; Agent Miles, Report, **Annual Report of Commissioner of Indian Affairs** (Department Edition, Washington, D.C.), p. 59, 1879 (hereinafter cited as ARCIA, date); Acting Agent Campbell to Commissioner Hayt, May 22, 1879, NAOIA, RG 75, letters received, Cheyenne and Arapaho, 1879.

18 Howling Wolf to Pratt, June 5, 1879, Pratt Papers.

19 Agent Miles, Report, ARCIA, 1879, p. 59; 1881, p. 67.

20 10th Census of the U.S. (see note 15); list of indebtedness outstanding, July, 1881, OHSIA, letterpress copy book, Cheyenne-Arapaho Agency, Sept. 2, 1881–Feb. 2, 1882, pp. 156-59.

21 **Cheyenne Transporter,** II, No. 19 (May 25, 1881) [5]; Agent Miles, report to Pratt, ARCIA, 1881, p. 193; Mason D. Pratt to family, July 10, 1882, Pratt Papers.

22 "This Reminds Us," **Daily Herald** (El Reno, Okla.), Apr. 24, 1893 [2]; **Cheyenne Transporter,** V, No. 14 (Apr. 13, 1884) [1]; Petersen, **Plains Anthropologist,** IX, No. 25 (Aug. 1964), p. 154; George Bird Grinnell, **The Fighting Cheyennes** (New York, 1915), p. 310; Agent Miles to Commissioner Smith, July 10, 1874, NAOIA, RG 75, letters received, Upper Arkansas Agency, 1874, M839.

23 Petersen, **Plains Anthropologist,** Table 1, p. 162; Agent Miles to Pratt, May 23, 1878, Pratt Papers; Agent Miles, Reports, ARCIA, 1878, p. 55; 1879, p. 59; 1880, p. 69; 1881, p. 68; 1882, p. 57; Miles to Commissioner Trowbridge, Aug. 18, 1880, NAOIA, RG 75, letters received, Cheyenne and Arapaho, 1880, M1775; Record of Indian Police [1884–1886], NAOIA, RG 75, Statistics Division; Dyer, Report, ARCIA, 1884, pp. 76, 72.

24 Sheridan, Report to the President, July 24, 1885, 49th Congress, 1st Session, **House of Representatives Executive Document** No. 1, Part II, Vol. I (Serial 2369) (Washington, D.C., 1885), p. 65; Lee, Report, ARCIA, 1886, pp. 114, 119, 123.

25 Williams, Reports, ARCIA, 1887, p. 74; 1888, p. 93; Ashley, **ibid.,** 1889, p. 186; 1890, p. 180; Dyer, **ibid.,** 1885, p. 76; Lee, **ibid.,** 1886, p. 119; Sheridan, Report to the President, **House of Representatives Document** No. 1.

26 Ashley, Reports, ARCIA, 1889, p. 187; 1891, pp. 342–45; Commissioner Morgan, Report, **ibid.,** p. 44; House of Representatives, 81st Congress, 1st Session, Committee on Public Lands, **Fort Reno Military Reservation Lands: Hearings before the Subcommittee on Indian Affairs,** No. 21, 1949 (Washington, D.C., 1949), pp. 52 ff.; No. 2102, Howling Wolf, allotment file, Cheyenne-Arapaho Area Field Office, Concho, Okla.

27 Pratt, **Address before the National Convention,** p. 2.

28 Agent Woodson to Commissioner, Apr. 17, 1894, and enclosures; Judge Burford to Woodson, Apr. 14, 1894, and Indictment, June 5, 1893, NAOIA, RG 75, letters received, 1881–1907, 14950-94; "A Horrible Crime," **Daily Herald** (El Reno, Okla.), Apr. 22, 1893 [2], quoting the **Republican** (Watonga, Okla.); **Republican** (Watonga, Okla.), Oct. 11, 1893, p. 4; **ibid.,** Jan. 31, 1894, p. 4; "Telephone No. 41," **Oklahoma Times Journal** (Oklahoma City), Feb. 8, 1894, p. 4.

29 Woodson to Commissioner, Apr. 17, 1894, and enclosure; Burford to Woodson, Apr. 14, 1894, NAOIA, RG 75, letters received, 1881–1907, 14950-94; Secretary of Interior to Commissioner, June 15, 1894, NAOIA, RG 75, letters received, 1881–1907, 22885-94; F. A. Barde, **In Camp: A Description of an Indian Camp Meeting in Oklahoma** (New York [1911]), p. 19.

30 Barde, **In Camp,** pp. 19-20.

31 **Republican** (Watonga, Okla.), May 5, 1927; No. 2102, Howling Wolf, allotment file, Cheyenne-Arapaho Area Field Office, Concho, Okla.

NOTES ON THE PLATES

Note: Sources for the history of the Howling Wolf sketchbook (page 33) are: John Gregory Bourke, MS, Diaries, XXVI (Sept. 25, 1878), p. 25, the United States Military Academy Library, Special Collections Division, West Point, N.Y.; Edwin Van Valkenburg Sutherland, "The Diaries of John Gregory Bourke: Their Anthropological and Folklore Content," Ph.D. dissertation, University of Pennsylvania, 1964, pp. 13–18.

1. E. Adamson Hoebel, **The Cheyennes: Indians of the Great Plains** (Case Studies in Cultural Anthropology, eds. George and Louise Spindler, New York, 1960), p. 33.
2. George Bird Grinnell, **The Cheyenne Indians: Their History and Ways of Life** (New York, 1962), II, 4–5.
3. George Bird Grinnell, "Coup and Scalp among the Plains Indians," **American Anthropologist,** n.s. XII, No. 2 (April–June, 1910), pp. 303–04.
4. William T. Hornaday, 'The Extermination of the American Bison,' "Report of the United States National Museum, 1887," Sec. III, No. 6, 437–38, in **Annual Report of the Smithsonian Institution, 1887,** Part 2 (Washington, D.C., 1889). The italic description is also from Hornaday; Ben Clark's caption in the sketchbook read simply, "Buffalo Hunt."
5. Rev. Rodolphe Petter, "Sun Dance," **English-Cheyenne Dictionary** (Kettle Falls, Wash., 1913–15), p. 1029.
6. **Wooden Leg: A Warrior Who Fought Custer,** ed. Thomas B. Marquis (Lincoln, Neb., 1957), pp. 39–40.
7. John Gregory Bourke, MS diaries, XXVI (Sept. 25, [1878]), pp. 38–39. U.S. Military Academy Library, Special Collections Division, West Point, N.Y.
8. **Ibid.,** p. 49.
9. Grinnell, **The Cheyenne Indians,** I, 257–58. The italic description is also from Grinnell; Ben Clark's caption in the sketchbook read simply, "Antelope Hunt."

Set in Optima with Italics and Semi-Bold Heads
by Atherton's Typography of Palo Alto and Spartan Typographers of Oakland
Lithographed on Basis 100 Patina and bound
by Peninsula Lithograph Company of Menlo Park
Designed by John Beyer